© Safoo Publications 2021

Written by Amal Al-Aride & Dua Maczoomi
Illustrated by Samiullah Sehto and Amal Al-Aride

Preface

Surah Al-Imran

Indeed, the first House [of worship] established for mankind was that at Makkah - blessed and a guidance for the worlds. (3:96)

This book is intended to be an introduction to Hajj Rituals for ages 9 years and up.

For Muslims, Hajj is the journey that every adult Muslim must make at least once in their lives if they can afford it and are physically able to.

Millions of Muslims from all difference races, economic status, nationality, and sects come together in Hajj, each wearing the simple two-piece white Ihram clothes, this shows that there is no difference whatsoever between them as they all stand together to perform their Hajj.

During Hajj pilgrims perform acts of worship and it makes Muslims feel the real importance of life here on earth, and the afterlife, by stripping away social status, wealth, and pride.

Muslims from all parts of the world come together and show their love for one another and get to know one another without any barriers or obstacles between them.

The season of Hajj brings a great deal of good as Muslims come together and learn from each other. It is a chance to wipe clean the slate of one's mistakes in the past.

Going To Hajj
With Daddy

Hajj For Kids

Safoo Publications

This is Dua and this is her Daddy.

They are going to Hajj.

Hajj is a holy place in Mecca where the Ka'baa is, the Ka'baa is Allah's house.

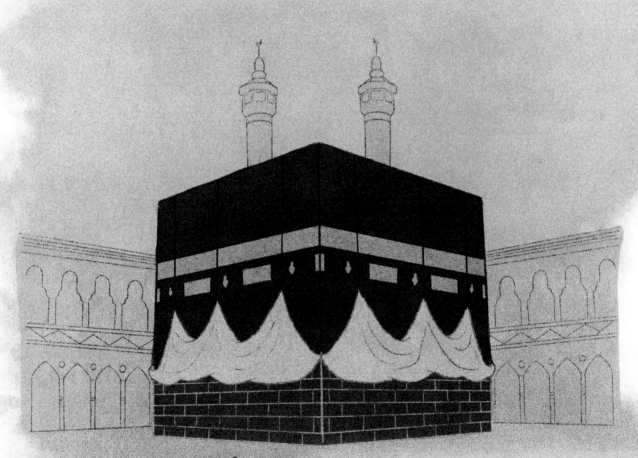

It's a cube that is dressed in black with gold decoration.

It's a place where all Muslims around the world gather every year in the month of Dhul Hijjah to erase their sins.

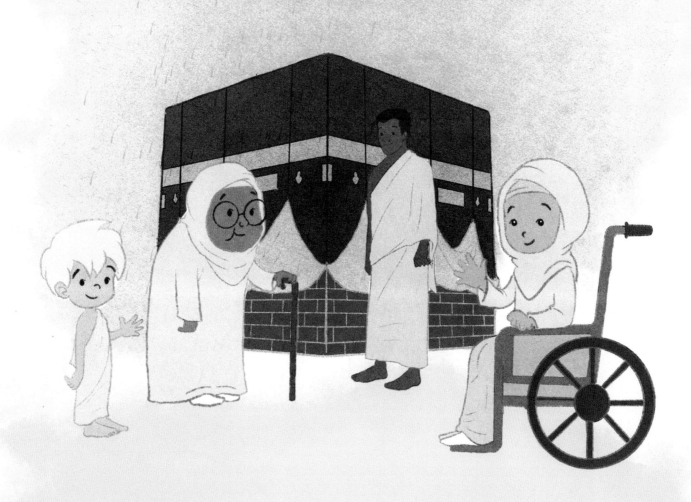

Dua has packed all the things she needs for her Hajj journey.

She takes the holy Qur'an,

her Dua Book,

her Tasbeeeh,

her white Ihram,

her white Hijab

and her prayer mat.

As soon as they arrive in Mecca they make sure they are all cleaned up and they put on their Ihram outfit.

These are their white clothes

Daddy and Dua then do Tawaf, this is when everyone walks in circles around the Ka'baa seven times and says "Labayk Allahuma labayk".

Everyone starts from the black stone and completes one circle once they reach the black stone again.

They then visit the Station of Prophet Ibrahim.

This is called Maqam Ibrahim

This is a glass and metal area with the imprint of Prophet Ibrahim's feet. This is where Prophet Ibrahim stood on a stone while he built parts of the Ka'baa.

Then Daddy and Dua run between two mountains called Safa and Marwa, they go back and forth.

They do this seven times, starting from Safa and ending in Marwa, just like Hajara did, the wife of Prophet Ibrahim.

After Tawaf is complete, Dua and Daddy cut their hair and nails.

Daddy shaves his head.

Allah (swt) tells us to do
this in the Holy Quran:

Surah Al-Fatih 48:27

Daddy and Dua then stand on a mountain called Jabal Arafat.

This is done on the day of Arafat

After this, all the people at Hajj feed those who have no food.

They do this by giving a sheep as a gift.

Daddy and Dua then sleep in white tents in Mina.

As soon as it's Eid, Dua and Daddy gather their seven stones and throw them at Shaitan, seven times.

They throw the stones in the direction of the 3 pillars.

Then they complete tawaf Al Haj and they do Salah Tawaf.

This is where they walk around the Ka'baa once.

The Route to Hajj

Mina

Stop at Mina to pray and read Quran

The white tents are where everyone sleeps

Makkah

Everyone begins by circulating the Ka'baa 7 times

Safa & Marwa Mountains

Everyone walks between the mountains Safa & Marwa

Arafat

On the day of Arafat everyone prays from the night to the morning

Muzdalifah

Everyone picks up the 49 rocks to take to mina for the next day

How It All Began

Allah (swt) told Prophet Ibrahim (as) to leave Hajar and their baby in the desert and this is what he did. Prophet Ismail and Hajar were all alone in the desert and they needed water.

She stood on the mountain Marwa and saw that there was water on the mountain Safa .

Hajar then placed Ismail in the area we call Maqaiam, she did this so she could see him while she ran betwen the mountains to fetch water.

Hajar ran between both mountains several times to try and get water, and this became one of our Hajj rituals.

When Hajar finally gave up on finding water she came back to Ismail and saw that Allah (swt) had placed water underneath him. She called it Zam Zam and they drank the water.

Printed in Great Britain
by Amazon